Our Nation's Pride

The National Anthem

By M.C. Hall
Illustrated by Todd Ouren

Content Consultant:
Richard Jensen, Ph.D.
Author, Scholar, and Historian

magic
wagon

Visit us at www.abdopublishing.com

Published by Magic Wagon, a division of the ABDO Publishing Group, 8000 West 78th Street, Edina, Minnesota 55439. Copyright © 2008 by Abdo Consulting Group, Inc.

Printed in the United States.

Text by M.C. Hall
Illustrations by Todd Ouren
Edited by Patricia Stockland
Interior layout and design by Nicole Brecke
Cover design by Nicole Brecke

Library of Congress Cataloging-in-Publication Data
Hall, Margaret, 1947-
 The national anthem / M.C. Hall ; illustrated by Todd Ouren.
    p. cm.
 Includes index.
 ISBN 978-1-60270-113-7
 1. Baltimore, Battle of, Baltimore, Md., 1814--Juvenile literature. 2. United States--History--War of 1812--Flags--Juvenile literature. 3. Key, Francis Scott, 1779-1843--Juvenile literature. 4. Star spangled banner (Song)--Juvenile literature. I. Ouren, Todd. II. Title.
E356.B2H26 2008
973.7'11--dc22
                                        2007034061

Table of Contents

Our Country's Song

Imagine you are at a ball game. You hear music. People stand up and put their hands over their hearts. Then, someone begins to sing. What is going on?

The song is "The Star-Spangled Banner." It is our national anthem. A national anthem is a special song that stands for a nation.

Where did "The Star-Spangled Banner" come from? Its story starts long ago with the War of 1812.

At War Again

America was once ruled by Great Britain. Then, there was a war between America and Britain. The Americans won. They started a new nation called the United States of America.

Years later, a war started between Great Britain and France. The king of England tried to make American sailors fight for Great Britain. This made Americans angry. In 1812, the United States went to war with the British.

Two years later, the war was still going on.

British soldiers burned the White House, where the

president lived.

Then, they decided to attack Baltimore, Maryland.

The British knew Baltimore was an important city.

Ships brought goods there for Americans to buy.

A Fort and a Flag

Fort McHenry helped keep Baltimore safe. The fort was near the water. It was shaped like a big star.

In 1813, the leader of Fort McHenry ordered a flag for the fort. He wanted it to be big enough for the British to see from far away. A flag maker named Mary Pickersgill made the flag. Her daughter and other people helped. It took them six weeks to make the flag.

Fort McHenry's flag looked different from today's American flag. It had 15 red-and-white stripes. It had 15 stars.

The flag was also very large. Each star was twice as big as a basketball! The flag was as tall as five people standing on top of each other.

Francis Scott Key

A well-known man named Dr. William Beanes lived near Baltimore. British soldiers captured him. They took him to a ship as a prisoner.

Francis Scott Key was a Baltimore lawyer. He was also a friend to William. He was asked to talk to the British about setting William free. On September 13, 1814, Francis went to the ship.

The British said they would let William go. But, they were ready to attack Fort McHenry. They said no one could leave the ship until the battle was over.

The British ships started firing rockets and bombs. Francis and William had to stand on the deck and watch. Everyone kept their eyes on the flag that flew over Fort McHenry.

The Rockets' Red Glare

Rockets and bombs fell all day. There was nothing the soldiers at Fort McHenry could do. Their guns could not reach the British ships.

Then night came. Flames from the rockets lit up the sky. Even so, it was hard to see the flag.

The next morning, Francis looked toward the fort.

The huge flag was still flying! Fort McHenry was safe.

Francis Scott Key was also a poet. He started to

write on the back of a letter. The poem he wrote was

the beginning of "The Star-Spangled Banner." It told

how he felt when he saw the flag still flying over the fort.

In the News

Back in Baltimore, Francis finished the poem.

Someone took it to a print shop and made copies.

The poem was called "The Defence of Fort M'Henry."

Many people read the poem.

On September 20, Francis's poem appeared in the

Baltimore newspaper. Now it had a new name. It was

called "The Star Spangled Banner."

Other newspapers printed the poem. Before long, people started to sing the words. The tune they used belonged to an old English song.

The song became more and more well-known. People sang it to honor the United States. Children learned the words in school.

In 1931, Congress changed the spelling slightly. It made "The Star-Spangled Banner" the national anthem of the United States.

25

The Banner Still Waves

Today, the flag that flew over Fort McHenry in 1814 is smaller. For years, people cut pieces from it. In 1907, what was left of the flag was sent to the Smithsonian Institute in Washington, D.C.

At the Smithsonian, people are working to preserve the flag. They want it to last for many years. They want people to see the banner Francis wrote about so long ago.

"The Star-Spangled Banner"

O say can you see, by the dawn's early light

What so proudly we hail'd at the twilight's last gleaming,

Whose broad stripes & bright stars through the perilous fight

O'er the ramparts we watch'd, were so gallantly streaming?

And the rocket's red glare, the bomb bursting in air,

Gave proof through the night that our flag was still there,

O say does that star-spangled banner yet wave

O'er the land of the free and the home of the brave?

—Original words to the poem by Francis Scott Key

29

Fun Facts

• The flag that Francis Scott Key wrote about was 30 feet (9 m) tall and 42 feet (13 m) wide!

• In 1814, all American flags had 15 stars and 15 stripes. The stars were for the 13 original colonies and the states of Vermont and Kentucky. There were three more states in the United States. However, the government had decided not to keep adding stars.

• In 1818, the flag changed again. It had just 13 stripes—one for each of the original colonies. It had one star for every state. The number of stars kept changing as the United States grew. Now there are 50 states and 50 stars.

• The flag at Fort McHenry was so big that Mary Pickersgill could not sew it at home. She had to spread it out on the floor of a large building near her home.

Glossary

attack—to start a fight against.

bomb—a weapon that is used to blow objects apart.

British—belonging to England.

fort—a place used to house troops. A fort is usually placed to protect an area of importance.

lawyer—a professional that is licensed to give advice about laws.

preserve—to keep safe.

Smithsonian Institute—the national museum of the United States.

On the Web

To learn more about the U.S. national anthem, visit ABDO Publishing Company on the World Wide Web at **www.abdopublishing.com**. Web sites about the U.S. national anthem are featured on our Book Links page. These links are routinely monitored and updated to provide the most current information available.

Index